Do You Know Your Self(s)?

*May you enjoy the journey
of exploring Your Self(s).*

Do You Know Your Self(s)?

Each "Self" Is Part of the "Whole" Person.
AWAREness Is the Key to a Healthy Alignment of All of Our Self(s).
SELF-AWAREness Is Living in the NOW.

Clay Dinger

Tampa, Florida

The views and opinions expressed in this book are solely those of the author and do not reflect the views or opinions of Gatekeeper Press. Gatekeeper Press is not to be held responsible for and expressly disclaims responsibility of the content herein.

DO YOU KNOW YOUR SELF(S)?
Each "Self" Is Part of the "Whole" Person.
AWAREness Is the Key to a Healthy Alignment of All of Our Self(s).
SELF-AWAREness Is Living in the NOW.

Published by Gatekeeper Press
7853 Gunn Hwy., Suite 209
Tampa, FL 33626
www.GatekeeperPress.com

Copyright © 2023 by Clay Dinger

All rights reserved. Neither this book nor any parts within it may be sold or reproduced in any form or by any electronic or mechanical means, including information storage and retrieval systems, without permission in writing from the author. The only exception is by a reviewer, who may quote short excerpts in a review.

Copyright for the image:
iStockphoto.com/lasagnaforone (Starburst)"

Scriptures taken from the Holy Bible, New International Version®, NIV®. Copyright ©1973, 1978, 1984, 2011 by Biblica, Inc.™ Used by permission of Zondervan. All rights reserved worldwide. www.zondervan.com The "NIV" and "New International Version" are trademarks registered in the United States Patent and Trademark Office by Biblica, Inc.™

Library of Congress Control Number: 2021945873

ISBN (paperback): 9781662918889
eISBN: 9781662918896

This book is dedicated to my mother, Hilda.

Mom, you have always been there for me with your love and encouragement.

I am honored to be your son.

This book is not intended as a substitute for the medical advice of physicians. The reader should consult a medical professional in matters relating to his or her health and particularly with respect to any symptoms that may require diagnosis or medical attention.

CONTENTS

Acknowledgements ix

Foreword xi

Introduction 1

Definition of Self 5

Chapter 1: Do You Know Your Self(s)? 7

Chapter 2: Authentic Self (Spirit) 13

Chapter 3: Intellectual Self (Conscious Mind) 19

Chapter 4: Physical Self (Body) 23

Chapter 5: Emotional Self (Thoughts) 29

Chapter 6: Social Self (Outside Influence) 33

Chapter 7: The "Other" Self(s) 41

Chapter 8: What "Hat" Are You Wearing? 47

Chapter 9: Morals and Values 51

Chapter 10: Values Review 57

Chapter 11: Is Reality Real? 61

Chapter 12: What Is the Ego's Purpose? 65

Chapter 13: Clay, ULC 69

Chapter 14: The Past, the Present, and the Future 77

Chapter 15: SELF-AWAREness Evaluation 85

Chapter 16: SELF-AWAREness Is Living in the NOW! 89

Chapter 17: Who Are You? 95

Chapter 18: Changing Your Identity 99

Chapter 19: I Am Me! 103

Chapter 20: The Traveler 109

Chapter 21: Wings of Pegasus 113

Chapter 22: Your Chapter 117

Chapter 23: Addendum 121

ACKNOWLEDGEMENTS

I want to thank all my friends, colleagues, and associates who read the first draft of this book and gave me their much-appreciated feedback. There are too many to list, and I don't want to pick one person over another. **Thank you all!**

FOREWORD

Do You Know Your Self(s)? is a new book that will offer you a practical introspective journey that will inspire you to look deep into yourself and all that contributes to who you are and who you want to be. In this book, Clay Dinger will prompt you to self-evaluate in a way that will enlighten you about your beliefs, intentions, and your own Path. It is also a workbook set up to help you put these new insights into action. I recommend this book to everyone who wants to get a fresh perspective and get started on a more meaningful and fulfilling life journey for all of your "Self(s)" working as one.

—Cal Banyan, President of the 5-PATH® International Association of Hypnosis Professionals and author of *The Secret Language of Feelings*

INTRODUCTION

I am a certified consulting hypnotist through the National Guild of Hypnotists and have helped thousands of people to lose weight, quit smoking, deal with stress, and many other issues that affect their health and quality of life. My mission statement in life is: "To make a positive difference in people's lives." Being a hypnotist allows me to do just that.

<u>This is not a book about hypnosis</u>. This is a book about learning how to become more fully AWARE of the different Self(s) that influence our decisions/choices in our lives. I have capitalized the entire word AWARE throughout the book to remind you that it is the focus of this book. Other words may also be capitalized to emphasize them.

While hypnosis can help most people, some people still struggle to make the changes in their life that they know are in their best interest. The original intent of this book was to help those clients that know what they should do but still choose not to do so. We all seem to have things that we know we should do, but we don't always choose to do them. As I was writing this book, it became very clear that just about everyone could benefit from becoming more AWARE. If you are a hypnotist, this book may help you focus in on how to look at your clients' problems in a different way.

When I started to write this book, I didn't know exactly how it was all going to come together. What I did know was that I wanted to be able to share my insights on what living in the NOW (the Present) really means. So, I decided to write this book for myself even before thinking about publishing it. Writing the book has helped me to become more AWARE of all the different Self(s) that we each have. It has also helped me to understand and explain things in a new way. It has absolutely been a spiritual journey and changed who I am.

I believe that AWAREness is the Key to a Healthy Alignment of all of our Self(s) in all aspects of our lives. SELF-AWAREness is living in the NOW and being mindful of the decisions/choices we make.

We all get caught up in the rat race of life, and we make many decisions/choices without being fully AWARE that we are even making them or why. There are many decisions/choices that we don't make and get frustrated because we didn't make them. Not making a decision/choice is allowing "Life" (someone else) to make our decisions/choices for us.

If we become more AWARE of why we should or shouldn't do something before we do or don't do something, then we could make better decisions/choices in our life. More about the word *should* later in the book.

This book is intended to help you become more AWARE of what influences your decision-making process. In other words, it will help you to understand why you make the decisions/choices you do, before you make them. It will help you learn to live in the NOW and be more AWARE of who you truly are—and, more importantly, who you were born to be.

Awareness is the greatest agent for change.
—ECKHART TOLLE

This book will ask you many questions that only "you" can answer by being more fully AWARE of all "your" Self(s) and how they influence your decisions/choices.

If you listen to this as an audiobook, I would suggest that you journal what each chapter brings up for you.

⁂

SELF-AWAREness is Living in the NOW.

⁂

DEFINITION OF SELF

In this book, I look at "Self" as being the particular part of our personality or character that we, as individuals, identify with through our behavior and action at any given time.

At the time of my research, Merriam-Webster defined "Self" in the following ways shown below (http://www.merriam-webster.com/dictionary/self):

Self (noun)

Simple Definition of Self

- : the person that someone normally or truly is
- : a particular part of your personality or character that is shown in a particular situation
- : the personality or character that makes a person different from other people
- : the combination of emotions, thoughts, feelings, etc., that make a person different from others

Full Definition of Self (plural **selves**)

1. a : the entire person of an individual
   b : the realization or embodiment of an abstraction

DO YOU KNOW YOUR SELF(S)?

2. a (1) : an individual's typical character or behavior
      <her true self was revealed>
   (2) : an individual's temporary behavior or character
      <his better self>
   b : a person in prime condition
      <feel like my old self today>

3. : the union of elements (as body, emotions, thoughts, and sensations) that constitute the individuality and identity of a person

4. : personal interest or advantage

5. : material that is part of an individual organism <ability of the immune system to distinguish self from nonself>

Chapter 1

DO YOU KNOW YOUR SELF(S)?

When considering the numerous definitions of "Self," it becomes apparent that the concept of "Self" may seem complex. I have chosen to look at the five (5) Self(s) listed below as a way to help explain how someone can become more "AWARE" of what influences their decisions/choices in life.

We each have an Authentic Self, an Intellectual Self, a Physical Self, an Emotional Self, and a Social Self. There are many other "Self(s)," but the main focus of this book will be on these five Self(s), Gut Feelings, and the Ego. Gut Feelings are the Authentic Self's internal Intuition signals that tell you if you are on the correct path or not, much like a vehicle's Global Positioning System (GPS), but we will go into more about that later.

The purpose of this book is to help you become more "AWARE" of your different "Self(s)" and how each of them can influence your decisions/choices.

- **Authentic Self** (Spirit)
  (Also called the Higher Mind, Soul, Intuition, or True Self.)

DO YOU KNOW YOUR SELF(S)?

- **Intellectual Self** (Conscious Mind)
  (Where we do our thinking and where the Ego resides.)

- **Physical Self** (Body)

- **Emotional Self** (Thoughts)
  (Thinking not based on logical reasoning.)

- **Social Self** (Outside Influence)
  (From family, school, church, society, culture, and so forth.)

The Intellectual Self generally gets to make <u>All</u> the decisions/ choices that the other Self(s) have to live with. So, it becomes very important for the Intellectual Self to be AWARE of why it is making decisions/ choices before it makes them.

In the case of the Physical Self, it has to live (or die) based on the decisions/choices that the Intellectual Self makes, such as over indulgence of food, tobacco, alcohol, drugs, etc. The Emotional Self and the Social Self can sometimes override (or influence) the Intellectual Self. Even the Physical Self can create cravings that will try to influence the Intellectual Self.

The Intellectual Self, and the other Self(s) listed above, cannot exist without the Physical Self and cannot fully enjoy life without the Physical Self being in good shape. When the Intellectual Self doesn't make good decisions/choices, the Physical Self and the Emotional Self may suffer.

So why doesn't the Intellectual Self make better decisions/choices?

We all have many things that influence what we think and do. Most times, we are not even AWARE that we are actually being influenced by the various Self(s) listed above. A lot of our beliefs were ingrained into us during childhood from our parents, family, school, church, society, culture, and so on. Sometimes, we are not even AWARE of the beliefs that we have. And yet, every decision/choice we make is based on a belief, even if we are not AWARE that the belief exists.

The concept of this book started from a conversation that I had with a hypnosis client who wanted to lose weight but wasn't doing the things that she knew she should be doing—like eating less sweets—even though her weight and Type II Diabetes were getting worse. She was getting frustrated not only with the lack of results but with herself for not being able to make the changes that she knew were in her best interest.

I started our conversation by saying, "You have an Intellectual Self and a Physical Self. And the Intellectual Self gets to make all the decisions/choices around what to eat or not eat, what to drink or not drink, and whether to exercise or not exercise. Consequently, the Physical Self has to live (or die) based on the decisions/choices that the Intellectual Self makes. So you would think (purely from a logical standpoint) that the Intellectual Self would make better decisions/choices because it needs the Physical Self in order to exist. The Intellectual Self needs the Physical Self to be in good shape so that the Intellectual Self can fully enjoy life. So why doesn't the Intellectual Self make better decisions/choices? Perhaps it is because the Intellectual Self is letting the Ego get in the way. When it listens to the Ego, the Intellectual Self loses its AWAREness of the Other Self(s) and may only be focused on short-term gratification." (Chapter 12 will focus on "What is the Ego's purpose?")

I continued on with, "Now, I am not ready to blame everything on the Ego, but that is a possibility. If the Ego is calling the shots, then it might be looking for instant gratification without taking the long-term effects of its decisions/choices into consideration. If the Intellectual Self could simply become more AWARE of the impact that its decisions/choices have on the Physical Self, then the Intellectual Self should make better decisions/choices. Even the Ego should enjoy having a healthier Physical Self."

At that point in the conversation, the client asked me, "Where does the Spiritual Self come into play with all that?" I smiled at her and said, "That's a good question, because I haven't thought about that yet. But I will absolutely give that some consideration before I see you again."

I believe that she was looking (hoping) for the Spiritual Self to be able to step in and straighten out the Intellectual Self without requiring her to do anything on her own. It was a great question, but I didn't have an answer at that time.

As I pondered the role of the Spiritual Self, I realized that there were two other main Self(s) that could impact our decisions/choices: the Emotional Self and the Social Self. I concluded that those five different Self(s) are like different points on a star that represents the "Whole" person.

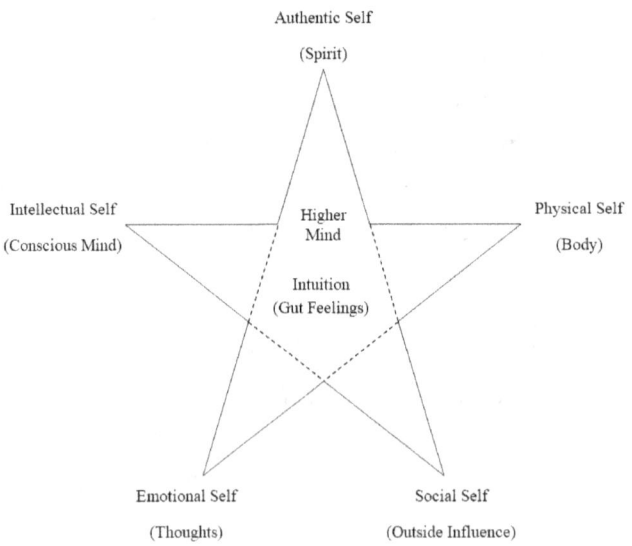

AWAREness is being "Mindful" of our Authentic Self, Intellectual Self, Physical Self, Emotional Self, Social Self, and Ego when making decisions/choices. Each Self is part of the "Whole" person. Although I reference weight loss above, <u>becoming fully AWARE of All your Self(s) and how they impact your decisions/choices can be applied to any aspect of your life</u>.

By the next session, the client above realized that as a child both her mother and grandmother would use "sweets" as a way to deal with her anytime she was upset, bored, or sad. She was taught (nonverbally) that "sweets" were the answer to dealing with everything. This was not only a belief she had learned nonverbally, but also a "sacred" belief because it came from her mother and grandmother. With new AWAREness, she easily lost 65 pounds and reached her goal weight. (More about beliefs in Chapter 6.)

Throughout this book, I ask you to think about, "What is in your best interest?" or, "What is in the best interest of a specific Self?" This doesn't mean you should ignore everybody else's feelings and always put yourself first. It simply means being AWARE of what is "truly" in your best interest. Sometimes, when we make decisions/choices that we think are not in our best interest, and we do that out of honor and respect (or love) for someone else, it may well be in our best interest in the long run. So, being more AWARE of why we are or are not doing something can make any decision/choice more understandable.

***If you don't know your Self(s),
then you don't know who you really are!***

DO YOU KNOW YOUR SELF(S)?

THOUGHTS OR QUESTIONS CHAPTER 1 MAY HAVE CREATED:

Chapter 2

AUTHENTIC SELF (SPIRIT)

The Authentic Self is who we were born to be when we came into this life. It can also be referred to as our Spirit, the Higher Mind, Intuition, Gut Feelings, or even the Soul. Regardless of what you call it, the Authentic Self resides within the Unconscious Mind and has been there since birth.

For clarification, consider the various minds in this way:

Conscious Mind:
Where we do our conscious thinking from.
Can only keep track of seven to nine things at any given time.

Subconscious Mind:
Where every event in our lives is stored, like in a big database.
Also, where all our values, beliefs and habits are stored.

Unconscious Mind:
Where our Authentic Self and basic Morals reside.
Also, where our Intuition (Gut Feelings) is stored.

It is my belief that we are born with basic Morals and Intuition (Gut Feelings). We don't learn Gut Feelings. What we learn is to associate various Gut Feelings with different types of events. For instance, if we see something that makes us sad, we don't think about being sad; we are just sad. If we see something that makes us angry, we don't think about being angry; we are just angry. Sometimes, we unintentionally "link" those events to a specific Gut Feeling. When this happens, we immediately re-experience (relive) the Gut Feeling every time we recall the event. If we remain focused on the event, the Gut Feelings can end up consuming and even hurting us. (More about that in Chapter 5 on the Emotional Self.)

If something goes against our basic Morals, that can also create Gut Feelings. That is why I believe that we are born with basic Morals and Gut Feelings.

Part of the concept above was inspired by the book *The Secret Language of Feelings,* written by Calvin D. Banyan. I would highly recommend this book to anyone who wants to have a different perspective of their emotions and feelings, which are two different things.

The Authentic Self communicates through our Gut Feelings. Gut Feelings are similar to the Global Positioning System (GPS) used in vehicles that helps keep us on track. Sometimes, we do not listen to or even hear that inner voice, especially when we get caught up in the Rat Race of Life and let our emotions overwhelm us.

Our mission in life should be to find and listen to our Authentic Self. At times, we all know what we should or shouldn't be doing, and yet we still don't do what we know is in our best interest. When that happens, we are "not" listening to our Authentic Self and are letting our other Self(s) influence and/or make our decisions/choices for us. Your

Intuition is never wrong, although you may misinterpret it sometimes. Relying on your Intuition is certainly a learning process. Your Intuition is your "True GPS."

It is possible to look at your Authentic Self as an observer of what is happening in your life at any given point in time. When you do this, the Authentic Self then sends Gut Feelings back to you to let you know what is going on. This is how your Gut Feelings become your internal Intuition signals, which are designed to keep you on track and warn you of any possible dangers.

I have taught many people how to step from the front of their mind to the back of their mind, where there is an observation deck for them to use, to look at any situation without it being in their face. When you mentally step back to your observation deck, you are not running away from anything. You are simply disassociating (disengaging) from something so that you can see it more clearly for what it is "before" you decide what you are going to do or not do about it. We don't get to decide what life throws at us on any given day, but we absolutely do get to decide how we are going to respond or react to something. If we mentally step back from any situation and let ourselves see things more clearly, we have a greater chance of understanding our actions before we decide how to respond to the situation.

I once heard the late Dr. Wayne Dyer say, "Prayer is talking to God. Meditation is listening to God." Meditation is a great way to listen to your Authentic Self, particularly if you are having trouble hearing or listening to your Gut Feelings. Meditation is a way to get the conscious mind to be less critical and less analytical. This will allow you to more clearly hear what your Authentic Self is trying to say to you. Often, we ask ourselves questions but don't have (or make) the time to listen for the answers. Meditation can be a way to listen.

Try this quick exercise: Take a nice deep breath, and hold it for a few seconds … and as you exhale, let go of all the stress and tension that your body is holding on to. … Take another nice deep breath, and hold it for a few seconds … and again, as you exhale let go of all the stress and tension that your body is holding on to. … Now close your eyes (if you safely can) and repeat the exercise. Notice how it changes you. Notice how your body relaxes more with each exhale. It can also change your AWAREness and help you to listen to your internal Intuition signals, called Gut Feelings.

||||||||||||||||||||||||||||||||||||||||||||||||||||||||||||||||||||||||||||||||||||||||||||||||||||

Discovering your Authentic Self starts right here and NOW, so that you can be the person you were born to be.

||||||||||||||||||||||||||||||||||||||||||||||||||||||||||||||||||||||||||||||||||||||||||||||||||||

THOUGHTS OR QUESTIONS CHAPTER 2 MAY HAVE CREATED:

Chapter 3

INTELLECTUAL SELF (CONSCIOUS MIND)

The Intellectual Self (or Conscious Mind) is where we do all our thinking or lack of thinking. It can analyze, overanalyze, or under-analyze things.

The Intellectual Self generally gets to make all the decisions/choices that the other Self(s) have to live with. Bodily functions, however, may force it to make decisions/choices more quickly. The Emotional Self and Social Self can also influence the Intellectual Self. Even the Physical Self can influence the Intellectual Self if it develops cravings.

When the Intellectual Self makes a decision/choice, do you know why? Do you even wonder why?

In the previous chapter, I mentioned that the conscious mind can only keep track of seven to nine things at any given time. Have you ever walked into a room, opened a door or drawer, and stood there wondering what you are there for? I have done that many times. Usually, when you go back to where you were originally, you will recall what it was that you wanted or needed to get.

Here is what happened. When you decided you had to go get something, and you got up to go get it, your thoughts about other things started taking up the seven to nine slots in your conscious mind. When more than seven to nine new thoughts came into your conscious mind, what you were going after dropped out of your conscious mind. In other words, you very quickly forgot what it was that you wanted or needed.

The Intellectual Self (conscious mind) cannot always be relied on to stay focused. *This is why willpower doesn't always work*. There are often just too many stimuli bombarding the conscious mind for it to stay focused. The Intellectual Self is constantly being distracted with miscellaneous thoughts and stimuli that can make it hard to stay focused. For example, say you're driving down the road and want to remember to do something as soon as you get to where you are going. You know you are not going to let yourself forget this task. Then a flashing red light shows up in your rearview mirror. I would bet that you are no longer thinking about what it was you were going to do when you reached your destination. You may remember it, but you may not. At the moment you saw that flashing red light, your conscious mind was being bombarded with all kinds of thoughts related to the flashing red light, and chances are that you will temporarily lose track of the task you were going to do when you got to your destination.

The Intellectual Self sometimes starts daydreaming, which can also prevent it from staying focused. When you are daydreaming, be careful what you wish for and what you think about. *Thinking about something, positive or negative, sets intent.* Your thinking can actually program your subconscious mind in a positive or negative way. Daydreaming about positive things can even become a distractor (or habit) that keeps you from staying focused on what is important to you. (More about staying focused in Chapter 8.)

The Intellectual Self needs to be more fully AWARE of the impact its decisions/choices have on the other Self(s), especially the Physical Self. Logically, we can know what is in our best interest and still not do it. When this happens, we allow the other Self(s) to influence our thinking and our action or lack of action. Most times, we are not even aware that this process is occurring.

Your Intellectual Self needs to be more fully AWARE of the impact its decisions/choices will have on the "Whole" person before making or not making a decision/choice.

THOUGHTS OR QUESTIONS CHAPTER 3 MAY HAVE CREATED:

Chapter 4

PHYSICAL SELF (BODY)

Through the miracle of birth, we came into this life with a physical body. Think of our miraculous body as being a vehicle that our Spirit (Authentic Self) uses to move about in this life. We need to honor and respect our Physical Self (our body) in order for it to honor and respect us throughout our lifetime. If we mistreat or do damage to our Physical Self, our vehicle/body, we do not get to trade it in for a new one. We either live or die based on that damage. So it becomes extremely important for us to take care of our Physical Self (our body) because it is the only one that will be issued to us in this lifetime.

The Physical Self generally does what the Intellectual Self decides to do or not do, even if it is not in the Physical Self's best interest. To complicate matters, many times the Intellectual Self is being influenced by our other Self(s).

Our Physical Self can develop cravings for certain foods that also try to influence the Intellectual Self to make decisions/choices that satisfy those cravings. Cravings can come from a variety of factors:

- **We can crave certain foods because of a mineral deficiency.** For example, a craving for chocolate can indicate a magnesium deficiency. A diet high in refined carbs and sugar is not only void of nutrients, but they bind to minerals and pull them out of the body, which can lead to a deficiency.

- **We are creatures of habit.** We tend to adopt the same diet and lifestyle as the family we were raised in. Certain foods may invoke a nostalgic memory and provide a sense of comfort. Therefore, we can crave these foods, and not having them on a certain holiday or event would feel like something was missing.

- **We can crave foods we are intolerant to.** Research shows that foods that produce immunoglobulin G (IgG) reactions can last as long as 72 hours after consumption. This mild immune reaction, to a food, acts almost like an endorphin (e.g., runner's high) in our bodies. The immediate sense of reward caused by eating the offending food is followed by a sense of lack, thereby increasing the craving for the food that we are intolerant of. Since food sensitivities can be delayed, they can be hard to identify.

- **An imbalance of the gut microbiota (dysbiosis) or overgrowth of Candida albicans in the gut** due to unhealthy food, toxins, and stress. Candida is a yeast that is part of our microbiome. Sugar and refined carbs are the food source for Candida, so when this yeast overgrows, it causes major cravings for these foods.

- **Chronic stress.** When we are in a constant state of stress, the stress hormone, cortisol, is released. Cortisol stimulates fat and carbohydrate metabolism for fast energy and stimulates insulin release and maintenance of blood sugar levels. The result can be an increase in appetite and cravings for sweet, high-fat, and salty foods. The long-term activation of the stress-response system and the overexposure to cortisol and other stress hormones that follows can disrupt almost all your body's processes. This puts you at increased risk of many health problems, including sleep issues, weight gain, sugar cravings, headaches, anxiety, depression, digestive problems, and memory impairment.

Having a healthy relationship with food, and identifying why you have these cravings or keep going back to foods that are unhealthy, is the first step to overcoming unhealthy habits. Mindful eating will help train the Intellectual Self to become AWARE of what it is in your life that is holding you back from achieving your optimal health. Seeking guidance from a holistic nutritionist can help you pinpoint where your cravings are manifesting from and guide and educate you in the proper dietary and lifestyle changes needed to overcome these issues.

The five bulleted items and paragraph just above were contributed by Debi Bryk, NC, BCHN. Debi is a Board-Certified Holistic Nutritionist, Certified Autoimmune Paleo Coach, Licensed RESTART Instructor, member of the National Association of Nutrition Professionals (NANP), and owner of Holistic Nutrition 4 Health, LLC. I took a Saturday class for five weeks on nutrition that was taught by Debi. I lowered my daily blood sugar count by thirty points and lost ten pounds in the process. Weight loss was not the reason I took the class. I took the class to honor and respect my body. Debi's website is www.HolisticNutrition4Health.com.

The Physical Self lets you know when it is not being treated with honor and respect by becoming sick, diseased, sore, stressed out, weak, lethargic, or overweight. Carrying extra weight around can take away your energy, wear out your joints, and cause a lot of other health problems. These are just a few of the things that show up "after the fact" as a result of you not treating your Physical Self properly.

It is important to honor and respect the Physical Self. How is that accomplished? Here are the basics:

- Eat the right foods in the right amount at the right time. (Consume whole, nutrient dense foods and limit sugar and refined carbs.)
- Exercise on a regular basis. (Move your body daily.)
- Drink plenty of good, clean, clear water.
- Don't abuse alcohol, tobacco, or drugs.
- Get a good night's sleep.
- Manage stress.

We need to do whatever is necessary to keep our bodies as healthy as possible. **_It is critical to take care of our vehicle/body because we don't get to trade it in for a newer model._** We need to truly honor and respect our Physical Self so that it will honor and respect us throughout the rest of our lives.

Now, the Physical Self may have some limitations that prevent us from doing certain things or eating certain foods. _Be careful not to allow any limitations to become an excuse for not doing something_. When we have limitations, we need to be AWARE of what we can and cannot do, but at the same time, we need to honor and respect our bodies by doing what we can do. Check with your doctor, nutritionist, or physical therapist to fully understand what you can or cannot do, and then do what you can. Over the years, I have had a number of clients tell me they can't exercise because they stubbed their toe, or something along those lines. While it may be true that they can't do certain exercises, it is generally not true that they can't do any exercises.

ROI is a financial term that stands for <u>R</u>eturn <u>O</u>n <u>I</u>nvestment. Most people want to get a good ROI on whatever they do or buy. So look at eating correctly, exercising regularly, drinking plenty of good, clean, clear water, and taking care of your physical body as an investment into your future. You can have all the money in the world, but if you don't have a healthy body, you won't be able to enjoy it. <u>*It's your body*</u>. <u>*It's your future*</u>. <u>*It's your quality of life*</u>. It's also your quality of interaction with anyone else in your life. You get to decide if it is worth investing the time and effort into having the healthiest body possible. <u>*You get to decide what ROI means to you.*</u> I have seen a number of people not take care of their body prior to retiring. After retiring, their body was not healthy enough to allow them to enjoy their retirement. What are you doing to invest in your health and future?

All the other Self(s) need to be considerate and AWARE of what impact their influence will have on the Physical Self. Since the Intellectual Self is ultimately in charge of making any decisions/choices, it needs to be AWARE of any influence that the other Self(s) are trying to impose on it.

AWAREness does not mean "not" listening to the other Self(s). It means taking into consideration what they are saying "before" making a decision/choice because there can be knowledge and wisdom in whatever they are trying to convey.

The Physical Self has to live (or die) based on the decisions/choices that the Intellectual Self makes.

THOUGHTS OR QUESTIONS CHAPTER 4 MAY HAVE CREATED:

Chapter 5

EMOTIONAL SELF (THOUGHTS)

The Emotional Self originates from our thinking about our thoughts and Gut Feelings. Thoughts and Gut Feelings can come and go in an instant. It's when we start _overthinking_ about our thoughts and Gut Feelings that our emotions can get out of control. When that happens, we give more power to the Emotional Self. When we let ourselves become stressed out, upset, anxious, worried, or overwhelmed, we are just adding more fuel to the fire beneath our emotions. This creates a great deal of influence on the Intellectual Self and causes it to make decisions/choices that are not always in the best interest of the Physical Self. The Emotional Self can also suffer from the decisions/choices that the Intellectual Self makes.

The fear created from past experiences can easily influence the Emotional Self. There can be wisdom in those fearful thoughts, and that knowledge may need to be taken into consideration to become fully AWARE of what the best decision/choice should be in any given circumstance. However, fear can also be a "learned or conditioned response" and become a habit. When fear becomes a conditioned response from past experiences, it is not a good thing. For example: losing the ability to trust others due to one failed relationship;

or wanting to be alone or lonely so you won't get your feelings hurt again.

Gut Feelings may initiate thoughts about something because the Authentic Self is trying to tell us something important. All Gut Feelings are good because they are the Authentic Self's internal Intuition signals. It's when we let our Emotional Self become consumed over our Gut Feelings that problems can be created. If you find yourself being consumed with a specific feeling, you need to disengage from your mind chatter and check in with all your Self(s). (Chapter 8, "What Hat Are You Wearing," can help you learn to disengage.)

Our thinking can sometimes masquerade as Gut Feelings. For instance, we get a Gut Feeling of sadness. Then we start thinking about how sad something is. We may let that sadness consume and overwhelm us. The Gut Feeling of sadness was just the Authentic Self letting us know what was going on. The Gut Feeling of sadness was our internal Intuition signal. That is what started us thinking about something that was sad. If we keep thinking about being sad, it can put us into an emotional state. It's our thinking or thoughts that are consuming us, not the initial Gut Feeling itself.

You cannot have an emotion without first having a thought, because all emotions are the offspring of your thinking. Alter your thinking, and you alter your emotions. Emotions may come and go in an instant. We get to decide how long they stick around.

Here's something to ponder: All emotions come from our perceptions. Our perceptions are what we think we believe. When we change our perceptions, we change our thoughts, and our thoughts create our reality. (Chapter 11 will explore the concept of "Is Reality Real?")

Thoughts can be debilitating or motivational. Thoughts can make you excited or depressed. Egotistical thoughts can sometimes be inspiring. But thoughts are just thoughts unless you turn them into Action.

Daydreaming can become a major distraction, and it may lead to procrastination. Sometimes this is good, and sometimes it is bad. If you spend all your time daydreaming, you are <u>not</u> living in the NOW. You are <u>not</u> being SELF-AWARE.

If you don't like your emotions, change your thinking.

DO YOU KNOW YOUR SELF(S)?

THOUGHTS OR QUESTIONS CHAPTER 5 MAY HAVE CREATED:

Chapter 6

SOCIAL SELF (OUTSIDE INFLUENCE)

The Social Self is what we think (believe) everyone else thinks (believes) we should be and do. For various reasons, we do make decisions/choices based on these outside influences, even when we feel (or know) that it is not in our best interest. The Social Self is based on everything we have learned (from everyone else) throughout our lives, particularly from birth through age seven. We have learned many things from our parents, family, schools, churches, societies, and cultures. As children, we look at grown-ups as gods. They taught us beliefs both verbally and nonverbally. We may not even be AWARE of where we learned some of our strongest beliefs. We all have beliefs (mindsets) that we don't even know we have. For example: do you ever find yourself doing something or thinking the same way your parents did, and you realize you have never asked yourself if there is a better way? You just do it their way without questioning or even thinking about it.

The Social Self may try to influence or override your Authentic Self's internal Intuition signals (Gut Feelings). It does not do this out of malice; rather, the Social Self is simply trying to tell you what it believes is in your best interest. The Social Self is just conveying what it has learned from "everyone else" over the years, and what it has learned is not always in your best interest. For example: emotional eating of comfort food when we feel lonely or sad. On the other hand, in some cases it may well be worth listening to your Social Self.

Because my father was an alcoholic, my mother taught me to avoid conflict at all costs. She did this without ever saying a single word. She didn't even know that she was teaching me a lesson, and I didn't know that I was learning a lesson and held it as a belief. When my father would come home drunk, which was most of the time, my mother would find some way to get my two younger sisters and me out of the living room. Like "let's go into the kitchen and make some fudge, brownies, cookies, popcorn, or anything" that required us to get out of the living room.

When I got out of the Air Force at age twenty-two, I got a job as a computer operator and within one year became manager of the Data Processing department. That is certainly dating myself. As a department manager, I had to deal with all the problems of the department, including disciplining, hiring, and firing people. Back then, I was not a good manager because I would avoid conflict at all costs. I did this without ever realizing it. When someone came to me with a problem, I would address it with them, but in my mind, I was always thinking (and hoping) that it would go away tomorrow. However, problems don't go away by wishing they would disappear, and they only get bigger when avoided.

It was probably ten years later that a friend of mine brought to my attention that I may have learned the avoidance lesson from my mother. The light bulb went off in my mind, and my life completely changed. I started looking for conflict in the department. Conflict meant that there was something not quite right, and it represented the opportunity to make something better. I became a much better manager after that.

Martha Beck's book on *Finding Your Own North Star* says that we were born with an "Essential Self" and that we end up developing a "Social Self" that may be in conflict with the "Essential Self." If you read her book, please take the time to do the valuable exercises for each chapter.

Trying to be or do what other people think you should be or do can affect your Intellectual Self, your Physical Self, and your Emotional Self, and go against your Authentic Self.

Do you worry about what others think about you? We all do this from time to time without even realizing that we are doing it. It's when we let that worry consume us that it becomes a problem. Instead of worrying about what others think of us, we should be thinking about what is in our best interest. Doing something for others that we don't really want to do may in fact be in our best interest in the long run. For example, volunteer work that benefits the community may seem like a lot of work, but it may also reveal how wonderful you are as a person and how valuable you are as a community contributor.

A word of caution: our Strength can be our Weakness and our Weakness can be our Strength. The stronger we believe in something, the more limiting it may be. If we believe so very strongly in something, we may not be open to learning or exploring new ideas or concepts that might expand beyond that belief. The stronger we believe in something, the more we may be putting a box around it as a belief, especially when the Ego is involved. That box may limit your thoughts and imagination and prevent any new information from becoming part of your AWAREness. If we don't have a strong belief about something, we are more apt to want to learn and explore new ideas and concepts. This would be where a weakness could become a strength in wanting to learn more. (More about the Ego in Chapter 12.)

Beliefs need to be challenged for us to become more AWARE of which decisions/choices are going to be in our best interest. So when you think about your beliefs, both the known and unknown, ask yourself: Is this "my" belief? Where did it come from? If somebody else believes something else, are they wrong? If I believe something else, am I wrong? Have I really thought about what this belief means? Have I explored the limits of this belief? Do I even understand this belief? Is this belief holding me back in some way? Take some time to really consider these questions, which are repeated at end of this chapter.

When you hear yourself say, "I can't do that," ask yourself from where or whom did that belief come? Is that really my belief, or is it something someone told me when I was younger? Is this belief actually true?

The Social Self is generally a reflection of "learned behaviors" from other people as you grew up. Who did you learn them from? Were they good lessons? Is what you learned really in your best interest, and does it still apply today?

What is your dream, and is it really *"your"* dream? Or is your dream what you perceive that other people think it should be? Be honest with yourself when you answer that question.

Are you holding yourself to someone else's standards and/or expectations?

Who placed your limitations on you? Your parents, family, friends, school, church, society, culture, or yourself? Those limitations can be removed if you expand your SELF-AWAREness.

Peer pressure can be another major influence on the decisions/choices that you make. Be careful (AWARE) of allowing peer pressure to be the major factor in your decision-making process.

What worked for you as a child may not work for you as an adult. You have grown up and now need to outgrow any negative beliefs or behaviors that you learned as a child!

AWAREness is not the same thing as a belief.
You can "accept" something for what it "appears" to be
and not hold it as a belief.

QUESTIONS ABOUT BELIEFS THAT YOU MAY WANT TO EXPLORE:

Is this "my" belief?

....

Where did it come from?

....

If somebody else believes something else, are they wrong?

....

If I believe something else, am I wrong?

....

Have I really thought about what this belief means?

....

Have I explored the limits of this belief?

....

Do I even understand this belief?

....

Is this belief holding me back in some way?

....

Is this belief actually true?

....

OTHER QUESTIONS TO CONSIDER FROM THIS CHAPTER:

What is your dream, and is it really *"your"* dream?

....

Or is your dream what you perceive other people think it should be?

....

Are you holding yourself to someone else's standards and/or expectations?

....

Who placed your limitations on you?

....

Was it your parents, family, friends, school, church, society, culture, or yourself?

....

THOUGHTS OR QUESTIONS CHAPTER 6 MAY HAVE CREATED:

Chapter 7

THE "OTHER" SELF(S)

When we take on the role of an "Other" Self, we automatically shift our thinking. We tend to act out in a way that we think that role should act. Most "Other" Self(s) are actually a form of the Social Self. They come from what we believe that particular "Other" Self "thinks" it should be doing or acting in a certain way at any given time.

Many times, we shift into an "Other" Self without even knowing we do it. We may have programmed ourselves to act in certain ways out of self-defense or even out of love. What "Other" Self did you take on today? What shift occurred when you did that? Is that shift in your best interest? Is that shift in the best interest of other people?

When I ask, "What's in your best interest?" I don't mean that you should ignore other people's interests. As I have said before, doing something for others that we really don't want to do may in fact be in our best interest in the long run. Becoming more fully AWARE of what role (the "Other" Self) you have shifted into will help you make better decisions/choices that are in the best interest of all involved.

DO YOU KNOW YOUR SELF(S)?

Below are some "Other" Self(s) I have identified. (There are many more than what are listed here.)

Parent	CEO	Compassionate	Doctor
Child	President	Loveable	Lawyer
Adult	Vice President	Compliant	Police officer
Sister	Manager	Sarcastic	Soldier
Brother	Supervisor	Defiant	Minister
Grandparent	Employee	Vindictive	Teacher
Spouse	Unemployed	Self-saboteur	Student
Partner	Retired	Inner critic	Waitress
Lover	Coach	Inner child	Janitor
Friend	Team player	Complainer	Author
Enemy	Volunteer	Pleaser	Overachiever
Victim	Caregiver	Drinker	Gambler
Abuser	Protector	Smoker	Underachiever
Bystander	Believer	Agnostic	Procrastinator

- What "Other" Self(s) can you identify with?
- What "Other" Self(s) give you an identity?
- What "Other" Self(s) empower you?
- What "Other" Self(s) weaken you?
- What "Other" Self(s) would you add to this list?

Each time we take on the role of an "Other" Self, we become a different person. Some people call this "wearing different hats." That does not mean that it is a bad thing. Sometimes, we have to become different in order to do what is necessary for our and other people's best interest, and even for the World's best interest. For example, the executive may need to become a loving parent when they go home to the family. The minister may need to take a hard stand with a contractor who is not doing the work properly on the church.

As we shift into any of these "Other" roles, our actions and thoughts can be in conflict with our Authentic Self's internal Intuition signals (Gut Feelings). When we experience the Gut Feelings that this shift can create, we simply need to honor what the Authentic Self is trying to tell us and <u>take that into consideration</u> before we make a decision/choice. Gut feelings might include butterflies in the stomach, nausea, hair standing on end, and so on.

Remember, when we shift into these roles, we are using what we have learned about these roles throughout our life from other people. That may or may not be a good thing. Perhaps we should ask ourselves some questions: Who taught us what a parent does? Were our parents the best role models for us to learn what parenting is about? Would you recommend your parents' ideas to your children? The point I am making is that what we have learned about different roles throughout our lives may not be what is in our best interest or that of others.

Examining your "Other" Self(s) can be transformational and can do the following:

- give you a sense of Self-worth
- validate your identity
- challenge your identity

- help you to become more fully AWARE of who you are
- help you to become more fully AWARE of who you were born to be

Where and from whom did we learn what role our "Other" Self(s) should be? Should that be questioned?

THOUGHTS OR QUESTIONS CHAPTER 7 MAY HAVE CREATED:

Chapter 8

WHAT "HAT" ARE YOU WEARING?

In the previous chapter, I mentioned that taking on the role of an "Other" Self can be like "Wearing a Different Hat." Sometimes we are AWARE of this happening, and other times we are not. We shift into and out of many different hats during the course of the day and even during the course of a given minute. Each time we make that shift, we change our personality in ways that we may not even be AWARE of.

If you are focused on a task and the phone rings, you have the option of answering the phone or letting the caller leave a message. If you decide to answer the phone call, you will probably put on a different hat, unless it is your job to answer phone calls. If you answer the phone call, you will temporarily lose focus on what you were previously doing. If you lose focus on what you were previously doing, you may or may not get back to the original task at hand in a timely manner. The point I am making is that we can all very easily get sidetracked by even the smallest events or situations in our lives.

DO YOU KNOW YOUR SELF(S)?

If you find yourself getting off track (or lost in thought), here are four questions you can ask yourself:

- What "Hat" am I wearing right now?
- Who (which Self) is steering my ship?
- Is my ship going in the right direction?
- Is my anchor up?

You can easily get yourself back on track (re-focus) by wearing the "Hat" of the Self that you need to be in order to stay focused on the task at hand. The above four questions can be a form of Mindfulness, which is simply being AWARE of the present moment. Mindfulness is living in the NOW. This can also help you to disengage from your emotions when they consume you.

It isn't just about wearing the proper hat. You also need to "Act" the part related to the hat. If you're going to wear a hat, then you need to Act the part and take Action. Action requires that you Act and Act is the key element in the word <u>Act</u>ion.

If you are wearing the proper hat and not taking action, then for all intents and purposes you are just an observer wearing the Procrastinator's Hat. When you do that, you are just watching Life go by.

Putting on the proper hat "first thing" in the morning helps to set the intent to focus on the things that you need to do as you start your day. Even though that focus may change throughout the day as Life puts all kinds of distractors into your life. We don't get to pick and choose what Life throws at us at any given point in time. But we absolutely do get to pick and choose how we respond or react to what Life throws at us if we put on the proper hat to handle any given situation.

If you want to stay focused on getting things done, you need to stay focused on what hat you are wearing and the action you are taking. You get to choose the hat you wear!

What "Hat" Are You Wearing?

THOUGHTS OR QUESTIONS CHAPTER 8 MAY HAVE CREATED:

Chapter 9

MORALS AND VALUES

Morals, like Gut Feelings, are something we are born with. They help us to judge what is right or wrong and define what is ethical. As Jesus said, "Do to others what you would have them do to you" (Matthew 7:12 NIV). Morals can trigger different Gut Feelings when we observe something that doesn't feel right. We come into this life with pure basic Morals of what is right or wrong. It is our Values, which we learn from our social environment, that can sometimes override our basic Morals. We all have "free will" to choose or not choose our Morals over our Values.

Values, in their simplest terms, are what we value. They are personal beliefs that come from what we have observed or learned from our social environment. Values can come from examples that other people have set for us, or from watching television, even the cartoons we watched as young, impressionable children. Values are a Social Self aspect of who we are. As we grew up, our parents, families, churches, schools, societies, neighborhoods, countries, and cultures all had a major influence on developing our Values. We learn to adopt our Values to match what we see as we go through life. This can be good or bad.

Do you know what your Values are <u>and</u> how they influence your decisions/choices? Most people feel they have very strong Values, but they aren't very clear on what those Values really are or where those Values even came from. Values get absorbed into our minds and can be bad or good depending on the person's choice. Values are stored in our subconscious mind, and we access them without even thinking about them.

- Where did you get your Values from?
- Who did you get your Values from?
- Do your Values match who you were born to be?
- Do your Values hold you back from becoming the person you were born to be?
- Do your actions support your Values?

Our Values are not ours unless we accept or adopt them as our own. Therefore, any Values that have been taught or shown to us over the years don't become our own unless we choose them. This generally requires a conscious choice, but many times we have accepted other people's Values without even realizing it. As children growing up, we looked at adults as knowing everything and mostly accepting what they said or showed us as fact.

As adults, perhaps we should reflect back on where and from whom we got our Values and question some of them. I am not saying that all our Values are bad; however, some (if not all) should be examined, questioned, and understood before we claim them as our own.

Here is something to think about: ***any Values that we accepted as our own are really just our "perceptions" of what we think other people***

valued. Maybe their true Values were much different than what we perceived them to be.

I look at Values as being different than beliefs. Values are how you measure something, as in, "Does it have value?" Beliefs can be just thoughts or facts that we have accepted as being true without ever challenging them.

Do you value one thing more than anything else? If you do, this book is not meant to make you feel guilty about anything. This book is about creating SELF-AWAREness, making you more AWARE of what you are doing and why you are doing it. There shouldn't be any guilt associated with AWAREness, unless the guilt comes from going against your Morals.

||||||||||||||||||||||||||||||||||||||||||||||||||||||||||||||||||||||||||||||||||||||||||||||||

Do you know what your Values are and how they influence your decisions/choices?

Are your Values truly yours?

||||||||||||||||||||||||||||||||||||||||||||||||||||||||||||||||||||||||||||||||||||||||||||||||

DO YOU KNOW YOUR SELF(S)?

BELOW ARE QUESTIONS FROM THIS CHAPTER THAT YOU MAY WANT TO EXPLORE:

Where did you get your Values from?

....

....

Who did you get your Values from?

....

....

Do your Values match who you were born to be?

....

....

Do your Values hold you back from becoming the person you were born to be?

....

....

Do your actions support your Values?

....

....

THOUGHTS OR QUESTIONS CHAPTER 9 MAY HAVE CREATED:

Chapter 10

VALUES REVIEW

What are your Values? And why are they "your" Values?

Below is a random list of Values. Exploring them may help you understand what your Values really are and how they may influence (for good or bad) your decisions/choices. List your five (5) most important Values and why they are important to you.

Family	Friendship	Faith
Humor / Laughter	Honesty / Integrity	Healthy living
Money	Status / Stature	Reputation
Helping others	Volunteering	Community
Creativity	Learning	Traveling
Feeling loved	Loving someone else	Compassion
Respect of others	Courage	Honor
Overeating	Drinking	Smoking
Love of humanity	Social justice	Gambling
Spiritual growth	Power / Authority	Fitness
Competitiveness	Environment / Nature	Pets
Patriotism		

What else would you add? ....

DO YOU KNOW YOUR SELF(S)?

1 Value .... Why? ....
....

2 Value .... Why? ....
....

3 Value .... Why? ....
....

4 Value .... Why? ....
....

5 Value .... Why? ....
....

*From whom and where did you get "your" Values listed above?
Do your actions support "your" Values?*

THOUGHTS OR QUESTIONS CHAPTER 10 MAY HAVE CREATED:

Chapter 11

IS REALITY REAL?

What is Reality?
> It is your Perception of any situation.

What is your Perception?
> It is your Belief of what the truth is.

What is your Belief?
> It is your Opinion of what you think is fact.

What is your Opinion?
> It is your Logical Analysis of any situation based on your limited frames of reference.

Do you know everything there is to know about every situation?
> If you do, you are probably no longer on this earthly plane!

If your Opinion is based on your limited frames of reference,
> Then your Opinion is lacking in its scope of any situation.

If your Opinion is lacking in its scope of any situation,
> Then your Belief is not based on all the facts.

If your Belief is not based on all the facts,
> Then your Perception is distorted.

If your Perception is distorted,
> Then your Reality is not Real.

Therefore, Life is an Illusion,
> Because in Reality, nothing is really Real.

But do not fret,
> "<u>Everything Is As It Should Be</u>." Because it can't be anything else, other than what it is, at the moment.

An opinion is a belief that is based on insufficient judgment.
Your "Opinion" is based on your AWAREness of what you "think"
you know about any given subject.

Change your Perception and you change your Reality!
Your thoughts create your Reality!

THOUGHTS OR QUESTIONS CHAPTER 11 MAY HAVE CREATED:

Chapter 12

WHAT IS THE EGO'S PURPOSE?

I know a lot of people think that the Ego is a bad thing, but I believe that the Ego can be a good thing. It's only when we let the Ego control us that it becomes a problem. When we let the Ego decide/choose what we are going to do or not do, we are ignoring all our other Self(s), especially the Authentic Self. This can lead to emotional, physical, and self-esteem problems.

The Ego may like being "Liked" and do things to impress other people while ignoring what your other Self(s) are saying. There is nothing wrong with being "Liked" but sometimes you need to put yourself first. Always trying to please other people is a good way to ignore yourself.

The Ego can be motivating, especially if you understand its purpose. It wants to lay claim to something that makes it unique. The Ego may want the following: (1) be number 1 at something; (2) be the best at something; (3) have the best of something; or (4) make you feel that you are good at something. In many cases the Ego is just trying to inspire you to reach out for something it perceives as being better.

DO YOU KNOW YOUR SELF(S)?

The Ego, in many cases, can be like another Social Self that has been taught by others what would make it the best at something. The Ego has been taught that it should strive to be better than anybody else and that it is a good thing to outdo everybody else. In many countries, media marketing has been telling the Ego that the more it has in material things, the more important it is.

So given where the Ego has gotten most of its ideas from, don't you think that the Ego should be challenged? Or at least be taken into consideration along with what the other Self(s) have to say before any decisions/choices are made?

Napoleon Hill said, "The starting point of all achievement is DESIRE. Keep this constantly in mind. Weak desire brings weak results, just as a small fire makes a small amount of heat" (Napoleon Hill, *Think and Grow Rich*, p. 0).

Desire can be inspired by the Ego, but our other Self(s) need to be taken into consideration before any final decision/choice is made. What do we need to do to take action on our desire? Desiring something and not taking action on it is like (day) dreaming your life away.

I believe that the Ego resides in the conscious mind. This would explain why the Ego generally disappears when an emergency occurs and you are forced to think about the situation at hand. The Ego is associated with the seven to nine things that you can think about at any given time. It also tries to make each "Self" be the best it can be. If you let the Ego make all your decisions/choices, it can become a sense of identity, whether exaggerated or not, and it can affect your self-worth.

In some people, the Ego tries to be the worst of the worst. This occurs when someone tries to outdo someone else by letting everyone know that their problems, issues, troubles, and woes are far more terrible than anyone else's. So again, this would make it important to take into consideration ALL the input from the other Self(s) before making decisions/choices that are Ego-based.

***Be AWARE that the Ego
is just another part of the "Whole" you.***

THOUGHTS OR QUESTIONS CHAPTER 12 MAY HAVE CREATED:

Chapter 13

CLAY, ULC

This is the story of how I came to be Clay, ULC. Clay stands for my name, and ULC stands for UnLimited Corporation.

I share this somewhat unique and interesting story to explain how I came to a working arrangement with the Ego and all my other Self(s).

A few years ago, I found myself getting upset with my Ego and started talking to it as if it were causing me major problems. (In reality, I found myself getting upset with myself and started talking to myself while blaming the Ego.) I blamed the Ego because it wanted to keep getting better and better at playing computer games when, in fact, the computer games were just wasting my time and preventing me from learning or accomplishing new things. The Ego also wanted me to be doing more things for other people and organizations so that they would be thankful for what I was doing. Often, this ended up consuming my time with other people's problems or issues and leaving me no time for myself. I was getting a sense of satisfaction out of helping other people and being good at computer games, but many times it prevented me from doing the things that I needed to do for myself.

DO YOU KNOW YOUR SELF(S)?

This is how the conversation went. "Ego, you and I are about to have an impromptu talk. This is not meant to be a direct attack on you, but rather a serious conversation about something that is preventing me from being the best possible person I could be."

As I was saying that, I noticed a stick pen lying nearby. I picked the pen up and said to the Ego, "We are going to use the rules of a 'Talking Stick Circle.' When the pen is in the right hand, that is Clay talking. When the pen is in the left hand, that is the Ego talking. Whoever has the pen gets to talk, and whoever doesn't have the pen has to listen."

The Talking Stick Circle is a tool used in many Native American traditions. It allows all members of the circle to present their sacred point of view. The talking stick is passed from person to person, and only the person holding the talking stick is allowed to talk during that time. Everyone else in the circle has to listen intently to what is being said.

So, I said to the Ego, "Since I am the one who started this Talking Stick Circle, I am going to speak first. I am sick and tired of how you are constantly distracting me with things that waste my time. You keep putting things in front of me that keep me from doing the things that I really want to do. By wasting my time on things that are not important, you are preventing me from being a better person. You are preventing me from furthering my education. My mission statement in life is, "To make a positive difference in people's lives," and you are preventing me from doing that by directly stealing precious time from my life's purpose."

I rambled on until I couldn't think of anything else to say, and then I passed the pen to my left hand and let the Ego talk. Here is what my Ego said to me: "That's quite interesting, because you requested all those distractions that I have placed in front of you. And, if I'm not mistaken, you certainly have seemed to enjoy those distractions. So what's your problem?"

I was quite amazed at the response and thought that that was a very good answer and a very good question. The Ego continued on for a while and then gave the pen back to my right hand. I was still in awe over the response and conveyed this to the Ego. I guess I didn't realize that the Ego might actually be intelligent.

I further explained to the Ego that my frustration in wasting time with distractions is that it was preventing us from achieving something potentially great. I then realized that I had just referred to the Ego and I as "us." That started me thinking about the Ego and I "teaming up" to do great things.

There were a number of times in my life when somebody came up and thanked me profusely for something that I had done. Those times were always very rewarding, especially in an egotistical way. What made them even more rewarding was that I wasn't looking for a thank you or a compliment. At the time, I just did whatever it was I did without feeling the need for approval or thanks.

I asked the Ego if it remembered one of those specific times and how marvelous it was to receive such a thank you, especially when we were not even looking for it. The Ego remembered and agreed. I then asked the Ego if it would be willing to team up with me so that we could achieve greater things together. The Ego agreed. I then asked the Ego if it would agree to achieve greater things without looking for any recognition, so that when any compliment or thank you is given it would be even more rewarding. The Ego again agreed.

DO YOU KNOW YOUR SELF(S)?

Please note that the stick pen was being passed back and forth during all conversations with the Ego. Also, this conversation went on for many months.

I suggested to the Ego that we should run this team like a corporation. The Ego agreed but immediately asked, "Who is going to be in charge? Because your track record stinks!" When I got the pen back, I said, "Look who's talking!" At some point, the Ego asked if there were any other parts involved with this corporation that needed to be taken into consideration. That's when we decided to ask the Heart to come in to interview for the position of CEO of our corporation. The Ego wanted to call our corporation "Us Incorporated," and I wanted to call it "We Incorporated." We decided to let the new CEO name our corporation.

We then invited the Heart to come in for an interview. The pen in the right hand with the point down was Clay, and the pen in the right hand with the point up became the Heart. When the Heart came in for its interview, this is what it said: "Now let me get this straight. You're asking me to come in and interview for the position of being CEO of this corporation, which you want to call either 'Us Incorporated' or 'We Incorporated.' First, those names are stupid. You should call it 'Clay Incorporated,' or better still, 'Clay UnLimited Corporation.' Second, I'm not interested in the job. In all the years that I have been your Heart, you have never asked me for advice before. So obviously, I'm not qualified to run this corporation. Thank you, but no thanks."

The Ego and I were both taken aback by what the Heart had said. We were now left with no CEO. Although, we did like how Clay UnLimited Corporation sounded. We then decided that we would ask the Higher Mind to become our CEO. The Higher Mind would become the pen in the left hand with the point up.

The Higher Mind was also reluctant to be the CEO because Clay and the Ego did not have a good track record in getting things done. However, it also recognized that it was probably the best candidate for the CEO position. It reluctantly accepted the role of CEO and decided to hold a board meeting with "all" parts of this Clay UnLimited Corporation. It wanted "all" parts to have a say in any and all decisions.

At one of the many board meetings, a part of Clay that called itself The Creative One wanted to speak to the board. The Creative One became the stick pen held in both hands at the same time. The Creative One had been observing what was going on, and it made this observation: "All parts of this Clay UnLimited Corporation are stuck in the past. You are thinking like you did in the past. We need to find some way of getting everyone to be more in the NOW and become forward thinking."

Here is what The Creative One suggested: "We will treat the corporation like you would a computer. Each aspect will have an icon on the desktop so that everyone is recognized as a part of the whole. The icons do not need to be activated unless that particular aspect is needed. This will help us to stay focused on the task or problem at hand. Most times, we see the present through the eyes of the past and hold on to old baggage that may cloud our thinking. So, we will set up our corporation (computer) to automatically reboot and reset itself every morning at 3:00 a.m. This will turn off all aspects (Selfs), shut down, reboot, and check for any new updates. That way, all the programs (thinking) will be refreshed and allow that aspect of us to bring in the latest information it has, instead of looking at things through the eyes of the past. When an icon is activated, that aspect must bring forth its latest knowledge and wisdom with forward thinking."

That was a really powerful suggestion. Every aspect of Clay, ULC was in awe of what that meant and was ready to move forward with the idea. The Ego even made a suggestion that The Creative One become the new CEO. But The Creative One refused, because he said, "If you only bring in the new and improved aspects on an as-needed basis, you won't need a CEO. Every aspect will just be there as needed."

After many more board meetings, we decided that we would have an official ceremony for the compassionate unification of all aspects (Selfs) of Clay, ULC. This would be done to cleanse the negative energy of the past that no longer served us and bring in the positive energy that is for our highest and greatest good. This would be done with unconditional love for the highest good of Clay, ULC. Each aspect would have its own icon on the desktop and would remain inactive unless it was needed. When it was needed, it would be activated with all the latest information that would benefit the whole corporation.

The official ceremony was done by simply lighting a candle and setting the intent of what compassionate unification represented to all aspects (Selfs) of Clay, ULC. So each morning at 3:00 a.m., when we reboot and reset Clay, ULC, each aspect will have a fresh, forward-thinking mindset.

I sometimes think of this nightly process as a "Spiritual Dialysis." A cleansing of what is no longer needed and a resetting of any aspects that need to be updated with any new information or thinking from the previous day. So every morning all aspects (Selfs) are refreshed and up-to-date.

Side note: Two days after the official ceremony, I gave a talk at a local library on Stress and Self-Hypnosis. It was very well received, and many people waited to tell me how much they liked the presentation. As I was heading to my car, another person I knew also said how great the presentation was. When I got into the car, I said to the Ego, "Ego, what do you think about that?" There was no answer. The Ego was no longer a separate aspect of the whole. The Ego was simply part of the whole.

The Ego can be a great "TEAM" member
"IF" it becomes AWARE of the "TEAM."

THOUGHTS OR QUESTIONS CHAPTER 13 MAY HAVE CREATED:

Chapter 14

THE PAST, THE PRESENT, AND THE FUTURE

The PAST does not exist.

The only thing that exists of the Past is what you create in your mind at any given moment. And what you create in your mind is generally either the good or the bad part of anything from the Past. You are not creating the entire event or situation. What you are creating in your mind is most likely distorted and not necessarily real. (Refer back to Chapter 11 on "Is Reality Real?")

You may say that this or that did or did not happen in the Past, and you would be correct. But again, the Past does not exist. The only thing that exists of the Past is what you choose to remember or focus on in the Present moment. Staying focused on the Past sets intent on where you place your thoughts and energy. When you focus on painful events, you may also "Feel" the pain of that event somewhere in your body because you have linked that event to a painful feeling. That painful feeling is just your Emotional Self (thoughts) stuck in the past.

Everything is as it should be (right NOW) because it can't be anything else other than what it is at this Present moment. You can't change the Past. So, if you are holding on to anger or resentment, thinking that you should have done something differently, that somebody else should have done something differently, or that God should have done something differently, then what you are doing is <u>***creating fantasies in your mind about something that will never, ever change***</u>. You are holding on to the Past in a negative way and wasting your valuable energy and time by staying stuck in the Past. Remember: you can't change the Past so let it go. Start using that energy and time to discover what you can do to start living in the Present and move toward the Future.

If there was an injustice done in the Past, do what you can Now to make it right. If there is nothing you can do Now to make it right, then learn from it and let it go. Learn to forgive others <u>and</u> yourself. Forgiveness doesn't change the Past. Forgiveness opens up the Future and allows you to use the Present to move toward the Future.

Forgiveness is a shift in perception that allows you to let go of negative emotions or painful thoughts that are holding you back from being the person you were born to be. Forgiveness is acknowledging that anything negative from the Past will never get better. So, if the Past will never get better, why hang on to anything negative? Why stay stuck with the pain of the Past when you can simply let it go? Hanging on to anger and resentment of others is only hurting yourself and keeping you stuck. Forgiving others does not mean that you have to forget the lessons learned. *Forgive* and *forget* are two separate words.

Forgiving others is only part of the forgiveness process. Forgiveness of Self is just as important as forgiving others. Forgiveness of Self can help promote Self-healing, Self-empowerment, Self-confidence, and Self-esteem.

If you have been diagnosed with a disease or disability, then those are the facts at the time of the diagnosis. You cannot change that, but it doesn't mean that you have to accept the diagnosis. You can get a second opinion. If, after the second opinion, the diagnosis proves to be a fact, then let go of any anger and/or resentment of the diagnosis and start using that energy to find out what you can do to become an active participant in the healing process. Holding on to anger and/or resentment will only cause more stress and problems, and it certainly won't help you heal. Sometimes, illness can become an opportunity for spiritual growth and healing at a very deep and profound level. Start researching what other people are doing with the same type of diagnosis.

Since you can't change the Past, then thinking and worrying about what should have been done differently is a waste of your time and energy. It's what you do from this moment on that is important.

Most times, we observe and judge the Present and the Future through the eyes of the Past. This is generally done by our Inner Critic, which is just one of our "Other" Self(s). Our Inner Critic is that part of us that tries to protect us from ourselves by remembering all our past mistakes, failures, and shortcomings so that we don't repeat them again. Although this may sound like a good thing, what sometimes happens is that we start worrying that the Future is going to turn out just like the Past. When this occurs, we are still stuck in the Past, worried about the Future, and not living in the NOW. That creates undue stress in our lives. ***If you are physically in the NOW, and your mind is in the Past or the Future, where does that leave you?***

The Inner Critic plays into our fears and insecurities. But don't try to think of it as being all bad. In most cases, the Inner Critic is simply trying to warn you not to go there again. There could be value in what it is trying to tell you. But the value of what it is trying to tell you needs to be taken into consideration with input from all your Self(s). If you put a wall up around yourself, it can become a prison. No one can get in to hurt you, but you can't get out either. Pay attention to the Inner Critic, but don't let it control you. Don't let your Inner Critic steer your boat alone.

Regret is a judgment of yourself that can lead to self-sabotage. Remember, you cannot change the Past. Everything is as it should be (right NOW), because it can't be anything else other than what it is at this given moment. You may not like, appreciate, or even understand <u>What It Is</u>, but it is simply <u>What It Is</u>. So whatever has happened in the Past is just your life's experience up to this point. It's where you go from here that is important.

The PRESENT (right NOW) is the only thing that exists.

The Present is the only place from which you can make decisions/choices. You can't make any decisions/choices in the Past, since the Past is already gone. Those decisions/choices have already been made. You will make many decisions/choices in the Future, but they will only be made from a Future NOW moment.

The decisions/choices that you make or don't make today will have an effect on your Future and possibly other people's Futures. ***<u>Today is the Future you created yesterday</u>***.

Consider: that was then, this is NOW, and tomorrow is not here yet. What are you doing today to create your tomorrow?

You can learn from the Past and do things differently in the Present. You do not need to hold on to the Past when it prevents you from living in the Present or from planning for the Future. Spencer Johnson wrote an excellent book called, ***The Present***. It is an easy read, and I would highly recommend it for another simple way to look at the Past, the Present and the Future.

The FUTURE does not yet exist.

You can learn from the Past and make plans for the Future to be better, but you must put those plans into action in the Present for them to come true or be real.

No one can totally predict or control the Future. However, you can plan for what you would like to see happen. The Future is yet to be determined and will happen based on your decisions/choices <u>or</u> lack of decisions/choices made in the Present moment. If you keep avoiding making decisions/choices, then "Life" (or somebody else) will end up making them for you. This is called Procrastination.

I have seen many people say they will no longer live in the Past. They set goals/plans for the Future, but if they don't put their goals/plans into action in the Present, nothing will ever change.

Others think about the Future and still hold on to the Past. They say they will do this or that in the Future, and then they immediately think about a Past event that makes them cringe. This causes them to start worrying that the Future will turn out just like the Past. This can create undue stress about things that haven't even happened yet.

DO YOU KNOW YOUR SELF(S)?

You cannot find yourself in the past or future.
The only place you can find yourself is in the Now.
—ECKHART TOLLE

The only thing that exists of the Past, the Present, or the Future is the moment you are in right NOW!

THOUGHTS OR QUESTIONS CHAPTER 14 MAY HAVE CREATED:

Chapter 15

SELF-AWARENESS EVALUATION

Doing this evaluation will help you put things in perspective and make you more AWARE of which Self has been imposing more influence on your decisions/choices.

Please rate your AWAREness of each Self as a percentage, 100% being the highest rating. Base the rating on your AWAREness of that Self and how "it" tries to influence your decisions/choices. Also, please write down what you would like to change or shift about each Self.

If you have any significant "Other" Self(s) please include them also. And don't forget about the Ego.

% of AWAREness

.... % Authentic Self   (Spirit)   (The Soul, Higher Mind, Intuition or True Self.)

....

....

DO YOU KNOW YOUR SELF(S)?

.........% Intellectual Self   (Conscious Mind) ....

....

.........% Physical Self   (Body) ....

....

.........% Emotional Self   (Thoughts) ....

....

.........% Social Self   (Outside Influence) ....

....

.........% "Other" Self ....

....

.........% "Other" Self ....

....

.........% Ego ....

....

THOUGHTS OR QUESTIONS CHAPTER 15 MAY HAVE CREATED:

Chapter 16

SELF-AWARENESS IS LIVING IN THE NOW!

Now that you are more AWARE of your Self(s) and how they can influence your thinking and your actions, what do you do with that new SELF-AWAREness?

You integrate that SELF-AWAREness knowledge into your day-to-day behaviors and start living in the NOW while planning for the Future. Mindfulness is being AWARE of the present moment. Mindfulness is living in the NOW.

"To Know and Not to Do is Not to Know" (Stephen R. Covey).

"To be AWARE and Not Use that AWAREness is Not to be AWARE" (Clay Dinger, ULC).

Each "Self" is just a part of the "Whole" person. AWAREness is the Key to a Healthy Alignment of all of our Self(s). SELF-AWAREness is living in the NOW by acknowledging and understanding all our Self(s).

By being more AWARE, you can start making better decisions/ choices in your life. Remember that you can only make decisions/choices in the Present moment (the NOW).

SELF-AWAREness is a way to become whole by accepting all aspects of all your Self(s) with non-judgment, compassion, and forgiveness. Remember: "<u>Everything is as it should be because it can't be anything else other than what it is at the moment.</u>"

SELF-AWAREness will create an inner wisdom that will create a ripple effect throughout your life and the Universe as a whole. It will start you on the path of Self-Discovery and Self-Enlightenment. It will empower you to understand your decisions/choices in a new way that will help you to start taking control of your life and even healing yourself.

In this book, you have been asked many questions, questions that only "you" can answer by being fully AWARE of all "your" Self(s). Each person is totally unique and different, so there is no one magic answer that will work for everyone, unless that answer is: "Go within and become AWARE of all your Self(s)." Don't forget, "To be AWARE and Not Use that AWAREness is Not to be AWARE."

What is <u>your</u> dream, and is it really <u>your</u> dream? What outside influences have been shaping or changing your dream throughout your life? What is influencing your decisions/choices right NOW? Are you holding yourself to someone else's standards and/or expectations? Does your dream still match your Authentic Self's purpose in life?

I have a friend who has a daily morning meeting with all her "Self(s)" and the Ego. She consults with them for their opinions, concerns, and advice before she starts her day. This sets the agenda and focus on what is important and needs to be accomplished for the day. If something comes up during the day that is not an emergency, it gets noted and added to the agenda for the next day's morning meeting. If something does come up that is an emergency, then the appropriate Self(s) are consulted on how to handle the emergency. This is exactly how a well-run company or corporation would handle things.

How do you start your day? Perhaps you simply ask yourself, "What do I do today that is different from what I did yesterday?" Too many times, the day ends up being gone (before we know it) and we think to ourselves, "How did I end up wasting away another day?" When this happens, we aren't focused on what is important to us. We aren't listening to our Authentic Self's internal Intuition signals (Gut Feelings). We aren't being "SELF"-AWARE. Each and every one of us has 86,400 seconds to use each and every day. How are you using your precious and valuable time?

What "Hat" are you wearing right now? Who (which Self) is steering your ship? Is your ship going in the right direction? Is your anchor up? Or is your ship going around in circles or just sitting at the dock? When you find it difficult to make decisions/choices, remember to listen to your Authentic Self, as it is your internal Observer. Making "decisions/choices" is like using a rudder to steer your ship so you can make course adjustments as you move toward the Future and your goals. It becomes very important to understand who and what is influencing your decisions/choices. When listening to your Authentic Self, be sure also to pay attention to your other Self(s). There may be wisdom in what they are saying.

Who placed your limitations on you? Family, friends, school, church, society, culture, or yourself? These limitations can be removed if you simply expand your SELF-AWAREness.

DO YOU KNOW YOUR SELF(S)?

When you experience difficulty in making a decision/choice, here are some questions to ask yourself:

- Is this decision/choice in my best interest?
- Is this decision/choice in the best interest of all involved, including the Universe?
- Does this decision/choice fit with my Morals and Values?
- Do my actions support my Morals and Values?
- What will this decision/choice cost me?
- How will this decision/choice benefit me?
- Am I developing a sense of SELF-AWAREness?
- Am I listening to All of my SELF(s)?
- Which Self is trying to influence me, and why?

....

It is time to take responsibility for
  what you have done,
    what you have not done, and
      what you should/could be doing.

....

||||||||||||||||||||||||||||||||||||||||||||||||||||||||||||||||||||||||||||||||||||||||

It is time to Think for Your Self(s).

||||||||||||||||||||||||||||||||||||||||||||||||||||||||||||||||||||||||||||||||||||||||

QUESTIONS TO THINK ABOUT FROM THIS CHAPTER:

What "Hat" are you wearing right now?

....

....

....

....

Who (which Self) is steering your ship?

....

....

....

....

Is your ship going in the right direction?

....

....

....

....

Is your anchor up?

....

....

....

....

THOUGHTS OR QUESTIONS CHAPTER 16 MAY HAVE CREATED:

Chapter 17

WHO ARE YOU?

Who are you?

Who were you born to be?

Who do you want to be?

Wikipedia defines neuro-linguistic programming (NLP) as a pseudoscientific approach to communication, personal development, and psychotherapy that first appeared in Richard Bandler and John Grinder's 1975 book *The Structure of Magic I*. NLP asserts that there is a connection between neurological processes (neuro-), language (linguistic), and acquired behavioral patterns (programming), and that these can be changed to achieve specific goals in life.

Years ago, I took an NLP class from Michael Stevenson of Transform Destiny on "The Six Layers of the Mind" model. Michael Stevenson learned the concept of that model from Robert B. Dilts. I have studied and used this model to make positive changes in my life. Many hypnotists, myself included, use NLP techniques in their practice.

In writing this book, I have expanded this perspective and have come to believe there are actually eight layers of the mind, grouped into the three categories below, that determine who you really are. Chapter 2, Authentic Self, introduces the Unconscious Mind.

This chapter, however, focuses only on the original "The Six Layers of the Mind" NLP model. There is so much more to NLP then just this model. If you are interested in learning more about NLP, you can use the following link to access a Free NLP Home Study program from Transform Destiny.

http://www.freenlphomestudy.com/?a=1148

Unconscious mind:	**My perspective for book's purpose**
Basic Morals	You are born with Basic Morals.
Intuition (Gut Feelings)	You are born with Intuition.
Subconscious mind:	**NLP top 3 layers of the mind**
Identity	I am (or I) ....!
Values	What you adopted from others.
Beliefs	What you learned from others.
Conscious mind:	**NLP bottom 3 layers of the mind**
Skills/Abilities	Your potential or possibilities.
Behavior	Your actions or lack of action.
Results/Benefits	Who and what you have become up to this point. (Your Environment.)

You are <u>today</u> what you choose to be <u>yesterday</u>.

If you want to change your Results/Benefits (Environment), you have to change your Behavior.

If you want to change your Behavior, you have to change your Skills/Abilities.

If you want to change your Skills/Abilities, you have to change your Beliefs.

> This is especially true of your Limiting Beliefs, such as "I can't do that"; "I'm not smart enough"; "I don't have the time or energy"; and so on.

If you want to change your Beliefs, you have to change your Values.

If you want to change your Values, you have to change your Identity.

So, if you really want to make major changes in your life that last, you need to change your thoughts at the Identity level. To begin these changes, use the following process. State (say), "I am (or I) ....(this or that)......................................," and don't just give lip service to this statement. Say it slowly and with feeling in order to convey and emphasize to your subconscious mind how important this is to you. This is a great application for self-hypnosis that can help you reprogram your subconscious mind.

> *If I haven't said "I am (or I) ....(this or that)................!"*
>
> *How can I expect to be ....(this or that)................?*

DO YOU KNOW YOUR SELF(S)?

THOUGHTS OR QUESTIONS CHAPTER 17 MAY HAVE CREATED:

Chapter 18

CHANGING YOUR IDENTITY

In the previous chapter I explained how Changing Your Identity can help you change your Values, Beliefs, Skills/Abilities, Behavior, and Results/Benefits.

Simply saying "I am (or I) ....(this or that)........................." doesn't always produce the results that you would like, especially if you don't know what saying that statement truly means. This might be why positive affirmations don't always work when you don't give definition to what you are asking for.

When you say "I am (or I) ....(this or that)........................." you also need to know what your Values, Beliefs, Skills/Abilities, Behavior, and Results/Benefits are that support that statement. You need to understand what it means to Change Your Identity. It is important to know exactly who or what you are saying you want to become, and define what "this or that" truly means to you. If you don't define (clarify) what "this or that" means, how will you know when you have become "this or that"?

DO YOU KNOW YOUR SELF(S)?

The form below is one tool to help create (and understand) the results/benefits that you want/desire.

Identity (needed)   I am (or I) ....

....

Values (needed)   ....

....

Beliefs (needed)   ....

....

Skills/Abilities (needed) ....

....

Behavior (needed)   ....

....

Results/Benefits (wanted) ....

   (ROI)   ....

Your Results/Benefits are your Return on Investment (ROI). It is important that I am (or I) statements or suggestions are positive, in the present tense, believable, and focused on what you want to change. This is a form of Self-Hypnosis and is a powerful way to reprogram and re-educate your subconscious mind in order to make positive changes in your life. If you are going to use this for Self-Hypnosis you want to say the I am (or I) statement slowly and with feeling for 10 minutes a day for at least 21 days. You don't want to give this lip service so say it slowly and with feeling.

The following example was the first thing I changed using this process. I had been saying daily that "I am a daily exerciser" for many months, but the indoor exercise bike that sat three feet from my couch was only collecting dust. Saying something without definition was not working for me. It produced amazing and immediate results when I gave definition to the statement.

My example:

Identity (needed)	I am a daily exerciser.
Values (needed)	I honor and respect my body so that my body will honor and respect me, throughout the rest of my life.
Beliefs (needed)	I will live longer and be healthier.
Skills/Abilities (needed)	Identify exercises that will give me the results that I desire.
Behavior (needed)	Make the commitment to just do it.
Results/Benefits (wanted) (ROI)	A stronger heart, leaner body, lower blood sugar, lower cholesterol, more energy to do things, and being more attractive.

***What does saying "I am (or I) ....(this or that)................"
mean to you, and your future?***

DO YOU KNOW YOUR SELF(S)?

THOUGHTS OR QUESTIONS CHAPTER 18 MAY HAVE CREATED:

Chapter 19

I AM ME!

Clearly, each one of us can make the statement "I am me!" and know that is a true statement.

But what does that statement mean?

To each one of us?	To our family?	To our friends?
To the World?	To the Universe?	To the Creator?

Each one of us is today what we have chosen to be in all the yesterdays gone by.

Circumstances (even traumatic ones) may have influenced our life, but our decisions/choices were ours along the way. For whatever reasons we had at the time. We are what we are, at this point in time, and we can't change that. It just is what it is. We can't change the past, but we can alter the future.

DO YOU KNOW YOUR SELF(S)?

Using your newfound SELF-AWAREness, here are three questions (and sub-questions) you may want to ask yourself:

Who <u>am</u> I?   (What hat <u>am</u> I wearing at the moment?)
                        (What hats have I worn today?)

Who/what do   (Who/what is influencing who I <u>want</u> to be?)
I <u>want</u> to be?   (Why do I <u>want</u> to be ....?)

Who/what   (Who/what is influencing who I <u>should</u> be?)
<u>should</u> I be?   (Who/what was I born to be?)

As I said in an earlier chapter, writing this book has been a major spiritual journey for me. I thoroughly explored and answered each question and did each exercise many times. This chapter was most insightful for me from looking at my life as a spiritual journey and the lessons I learned along the way.

Wanting something can inspire the motivation to create the desire to make positive changes in your life. Wanting sets the desire to take action, but if the action is not taken, then nothing gets done and frustration can set in. Wanting sets desire to motivate, but wanting without action is not wanting at all. Wanting without action is just wishful thinking or daydreaming.

You can want all you want, but if you don't wear the right hat, you probably are not going to get what you want. If you wear the right hat, and don't take the action that the hat requires, you more than likely won't get what you want. Do your actions support what you want? If not, then maybe you don't really want what you think you want.

Wanting something, wearing the right hat, and taking action does not guarantee you will get what you want. But wanting something and not wearing the right hat or not taking the action will almost certainly guarantee that you won't get what you want. Whatever you want, you need to want it from your heart. What you want determines what hat you need to wear.

When I created my list of who/what I <u>wanted</u> to be, I realized that I wasn't doing a single thing to achieve most of the things on that list. So, the next question I asked myself was, "If I am not doing anything (taking action) to achieve something, do I really want that?" In many cases, the answer was NO and it was obvious from my lack of action. That helped me to focus on what I truly wanted, and that was to finish this book.

When you use the word "*<u>should</u>*," it generally implies that you are looking outside yourself for direction or guidance. There may be good advice out there, but remember to be SELF-AWARE when considering that advice. The only thing you "*<u>should</u>*" be is the best person you are capable of being. So perhaps the question you need to ask yourself isn't who "*<u>should</u>*" you be, but who "*<u>could</u>*" you be?

Your Morals or Intuition can also tell you what you "Should" or "Should Not" be doing. In that case, the "Should" is internal and coming from your Authentic Self. Again, that may be good advice, but remember to be SELF-AWARE when considering that advice.

Something to think about:
I am me if I wear the right hat and take the action that the hat requires.
I am me if I don't wear the right hat or don't take the action required.
I am me regardless of what I do or don't do.
I get to choose *who I am* by my actions.

DO YOU KNOW YOUR SELF(S)?

"Who are you?" "Who do you want to be?"
"Who could you be?"

THOUGHTS OR QUESTIONS CHAPTER 19 MAY HAVE CREATED:

Chapter 20

THE TRAVELER

*Am I done with my spiritual journey? Absolutely not.
I have only just begun my journey.*

We are but travelers on the road of life. Our final destination is surely death. So where we are going is not important, since we all must go there, sooner or later. What is important is experiencing the journey and hopefully enjoying it. For the journey is all we have in this life as we know it. In this journey, each of us will touch others' lives as we travel the corridor of time. Each time we touch someone's life, it is like a pebble being tossed into the sea of life. At first there is a splash, and then the ripples disappear as they reach out to infinity.

An old saying goes, "A journey of a thousand miles begins with but a single step." Every step is a journey within itself. Every second of your life is a step on that journey, whether you do anything in that second or not. Where is your journey taking you? Or more importantly, where are you taking your journey? How many steps do you have left in your journey of life? When you reach the end of your journey of life, will you have lived the life you were born to live?

None of us know how many steps we have left in our journey of life. So it becomes very important to utilize our steps intelligently and with purpose. May your newfound SELF-AWAREness give you clarity to see your journey's path as you let the light that shines within you also shine outward onto the world. May each one of us be like a candle that shines our light out into the darkness.

If this book touches your life, you will in turn touch someone else's life. For the ripple that was created cannot be stopped. It may diminish to nothing as time passes, but your life and those that you touch will never be the same. This happens every time we meet another person, no matter how insignificant the encounter. May the ripples from each of your encounters turn into waves that will carry your life to new and wonderful shores.

*It's never too late to **Enjoy the Journey**...*

THOUGHTS OR QUESTIONS CHAPTER 20 MAY HAVE CREATED:

Chapter 21

WINGS OF PEGASUS

Early morning sunlight, filtering through the trees,
Caressed each blade of grass, as it moved with the breeze.

The mist-covered meadow, was all frosted with dew.
And everything sparkled, as the sky turned to blue.

As I stood by the stream, with water cold and clear,
I thought I saw movement, but nothing did I hear.

I quickly looked around, and much to my surprise,
A horse came from the clouds, right before my own eyes.

With wings as soft as snow, he landed on the ground.
And though he was quite large, I did not hear a sound.

Beneath a willow tree, stood the horse with his wings,
Could this be but a dream, or was I seeing things?

I stood for a moment, not sure what I should do.
Should I run, should I hide, from this great horse that flew?

DO YOU KNOW YOUR SELF(S)?

But when his eyes met mine, the fear I had was gone,
And we spoke without words, in early morning dawn.

And then at last he said, **"Pegasus is my name.**
You know why I am here, and you know why I came.

Mount yourself on my back, and we'll soar to the sky.
We'll play among the clouds, and I'll teach you to fly.

But once we're in the air, there's no turning around.
You must fly forever, and never touch the ground."

But you have no bridle, no saddle, or no rein.
And if I were to fall, I would be in great pain.

"Put all your trust in me, and you will never fall.
I'll show you a new life, as you ride proud and tall.

Time passes quickly and, you have my solemn vow.
The decision is yours, but you must decide now.

For I may not return, or pass this way again.
And you and I are one, whether we lose or win."

The End or The Beginning?

May your new SELF-AWAREness be your Wings of Pegasus.
That will take you to new heights without any fear,
as you travel on the path you were born to be on.

The Wings of Pegasus poem was written many years ago when I was at a point in my life where I needed to "trust" in myself and that inner voice called Intuition. The poem helped me to lift myself up, soar to new heights, and never look back.

DO YOU KNOW YOUR SELF(S)?

THOUGHTS OR QUESTIONS CHAPTER 21 MAY HAVE CREATED:

Chapter 22

YOUR CHAPTER

Using your new SELF-AWAREness, this is your chapter to write. You get to choose how your life story begins from here. Will you remain the same, or will you become the person you were born to be? Every journey begins somewhere! Let your journey begin again, right here and NOW!

Some things to think about before you start writing Your Chapter:

- What story have I been telling myself?
- Whose story is it anyway?
- Is this the story I want to continue telling myself?
- Is this the story I want to live?
- Is this the story I want to be known for?
- If this is my story, then I get to decide where it goes from here!

Before you start writing, decide who you want to be and what changes you want to make in your life. Then write your story using present tense, as if all your desires have unfolded or manifested in your life.

For example:

I am so grateful and thankful now that ....

Be True to Your Self(s)!

Chapter 23

ADDENDUM

If you are still having problems making good decisions/choices, after reading this book, I would like to recommend that you find a good "Certified" Hypnotist. Even if you don't want to be "hypnotized," a good Hypnotist can teach you Self-Hypnosis. It is a great way for anyone to take back control of their life in any area of their life. In Calvin Banyan's book, *The Secret Language of Feelings*, there is mention of 7th Path Self-Hypnosis, which is a very powerful tool for anyone to use.

Banyan Hypnosis Center
https://www.HypnosisCenter.com
275 W. Campbell Rd. Suite 205
North Dallas,
TX 75080
(800) 965-3390

You can also contact the National Guild of Hypnotists (NGH) for a reference to a certified hypnotist in your area. Under the "Find A Hypnotist" tab you can enter your zip code in the Your Location box. Or page down and fill out the "Request Form" information and click on the "Send!" button. Someone from the NGH will get back to you with information on a Certified Hypnotist in your area.

National Guild of Hypnotists
https://NGH.net
3 Lesa Drive Merrimack,
NH 03054
(603) 429-9438

If you are interested in learning more about neuro-linguistic programming (NLP), you can use the following link to access a Free NLP Home Study program from Transform Destiny.

http://www.freenlphomestudy.com/?a=1148

If you have any questions or comments, you can contact me by email at Clay.Dinger@att.com.